Water and Other Poems
A Collection of Environmental Poetry

Water and Other Poems

A Collection of Environmental Poetry
Originally written in Odia titled *Pani O Anyanya Kabita*
by

Shatrughna Pandab

Translated by
Pratap Kumar Dash

BLACK EAGLE BOOKS
Dublin, USA | Bhubaneswar, India

 Black Eagle Books
USA address:
7464 Wisdom Lane
Dublin, OH 43016

India address:
E/312, Trident Galaxy, Kalinga Nagar,
Bhubaneswar-751003, Odisha, India

E-mail: info@blackeaglebooks.org
Website: www.blackeaglebooks.org

First International Edition Published by
Black Eagle Books, 2024

WATER AND OTHER POEMS
(A Collection of Environmental Poetry)
by **Shatrughna Pandab**
Translated by **Pratap Kumar Dash**

Original Copyright © Shatrughna Pandab
Translation Copyright © Pratap Kumar Dash

All rights reserved. No part of this publication may be reproduced, stored in a retrieval system, or transmitted, in any form or by any means, electronic, mechanical, photocopying, recording or otherwise without the prior permission of the publisher.

Cover & Interior Design: Ezy's Publication

ISBN- 978-1-64560-264-4 (Paperback)
Library of Congress Control Number: 2024939748

Printed in the United States of America

Translator's Note

As a translator of this collection of poems, I have been introduced to Shatrughna Pandab's poetic world of feelings, emotions, imaginations, unique experiences and a lot many things associated with fast degradation of our surrounding nature and its lifelike touch. The lost value of our natural habitat makes him lament. The loss is both in nature internal and nature external. In each of the poems, the poet looks like making a nostalgic journey from past to present. So, this translation is a kind of parallel creative journey alongside the poet in the art of interpretation, decoding linguistic and artistic literary notions vested in the source language, culture and creativity of the poet. While translating, the translator is in constant dialogue with the text to reflect its sum and substance in the target language and culture with approximation. It is apparent that the poet's journey abounds in the conglomeration of emotions, imaginations and experiences that are associated with nature, culture, and human attributes such as love, friendship and human relationship. Subject matters like praise of the beauties of the world; and the concrete things of organic sensibility of daily life also give vent to the material beauty. In addition, historical, moral, natural and socio-cultural themes constitute the essence of the poems. Much acclaimed philosophy of life, introspection, spirituality, social satires, socio-cultural consciousness, rebelliousness, changing perceptions of life, values and beliefs, focus on absurdity and above all the cross-currents of spatio-temporal thoughts happen to be the key concepts in composing such poems. Many a times, it is noticed that poet rejoices over fullness of life amidst the enriched scenic surroundings— implicitly, the environment in its truest and deepest sense. The seasons, the stars, the moon, the sun, the sky, cloud, flowers, trees, streams, rivers, waves of the sea, distant horizon, dusk to dawn, darkness and light, the quiet morning, the torrential rain, wind, the flowers, fruits, hills, valleys, countryside life, animals and birds, and even turbulence or snow fall in a literal sense have been put into the metaphorical matrix of poetry. The subtle senses of life's situations are ensnared in the art house of poetic mind and then they are painted with hue and colour which can yield stuffs of aesthetic relish. The poet is a dreamer; an idealist and deeply humane. His reflections on the countenances of life are nuanced all the way. Feelings are refurbished with the enamels made up of the chemistry of meditative perceptions of the microcosmic universe ranging from the embroidery of an anthill to the bluish merger of the earth and the sky or something more— all rejoice in the terrain of gifted soul of the versifier. The poet is an empathetic foreseer, performer, brooder and, what's more a rebel too. The holocausts of the past and the nostalgic reminiscences get in tune with the impulse of poetry protracting the sum and substance of their keenness of perceptions of the essence of life that moves ahead. The poet laments the loss because he cannot bear with the loss of the spirit of life on the earth. He cannot stay in the uninspired desert. He would rather look for the damsels in the oasis come floating in space carrying baskets full of sweetened thoughts. More adorable is the notions of getting perished. The playing of elegiac note of the harp of the poet not only echoes in the nerves of the humanity, but also sets an indelible whip to look into the mutuality of nature and human being which gets denatured with the potential roaring of the so called gallops of modernity. The loss of love of lily for the moon; the stagnancy of rippling-swaying-and dazzling sea weeds; the death of dancing of the buds and blossoms; and the feinted tapestry of unwavering cultural artefacts; and above all the loss of a sustainable life is unacceptable to poets. With these notions, an attempt has been made here to venture into poetic arena of the poet accepting the difficult business of translating his Odia poems into English written exclusively focusing on the loss of natural habitat and environmental degradation as a result of exploitation of nature by human being.

The poet looks around amidst palpable pictures; notices a flock of birds twittering, making aerial show along the beam of sunshine stretched sportively; a swarm of bees continue flying swinging from flower to flower – sitting on them, sucking honey and get invigorated to empathize the butterflies because they too flutter round them. The age old trees like the old bull stay stagnant but as a connoisseur protract upon the surrounding with the sharp rays of his eyes. At a distance, a couple of doves remain busy scrubbing their beaks. The arched cloud; the symphony of swindling and dwindling of branches of the thick trees; drizzling with the soothing air makes the tapestry greenery vibrant and makes all sing of the poetry of the earth which is 'never dead.' The glimpses of sunlight; the dazzling serene moonlit night; and the grinning leafy branches altogether cease to form the notes of harmony heralding 'Beauty is truth's smile.' The loss of all this indispensable wealth incurs unspeakable agony—irreparable loss of harmony of the being that constitutes all the life forms.

In the twenty-six poems, interestingly it is noticed that a multimodal rebellious voice or a sort of outcry artistically advocates for the surrounding environment that has been grossly exploited. It has gone to such an alarming state that the cosmic powers like the sun, the moon, the seasons and all the gifts of nature have become defunct hinting at the loss of natural traits of human being, and forecast sheer destructive consequences of this artificial life. The greedy and ignorant human beings have been destroying the irrecoverable surrounding natural wealth in such a way leading to unspoken disasters. Consequentially, the poems reflect on the dire need of water, wind, food, livelihood and many more things as a part of natural life and sustainability. What's more, his focus is on the denatured human being's search of the aesthetic notions in every aspect of natural life stands ironical. In this way, each of the poems carry in them rhetorical questions of our survival amidst the chaos of the bleak mountainous concrete buildings where many nemophilists get befooled.

There were a series of barriers for the translator while translating the poems which are felt to be mentioned here. The poems written n Odia carry their cultural, linguistic and literary typicality apparently for known reasons and that are associated with the language. While translating into English, there was dearth of equivalence of certain words and expressions. It posed challenge to render exact discourse structures as well as the original literary delineations of the poet for which a range of equivalence of the corpus have been formed somehow aiming at transcreating the poems. The words like 'jhila,' pejua,' 'phatakapala,' 'tadaga,' 'chita,' 'nanabaya gita,' 'adauti,' 'kaashatandi,' 'homakunda,' 'sathighara,' 'diparukhā,' 'ayusmala,' 'akulana,' 'ujaiba,' 'pilisaja,' 'jhanja,' 'nisada,' 'chandichamanda,' 'mafik,' 'panatakani,' 'dihudi,' 'jhingasa,' 'ghai,' 'shantha,' 'beada,' 'naanka,' 'apadebata,' 'dangara,' 'gemana,' 'madalasā,' 'chakrabyuha,' 'shunsef,' 'marāla,' 'krouncha,' 'nidāgha,' 'ghosajatrā,' 'unmehi,' 'kurei,' 'alsi,' 'antudi sala,' 'jhotichita,''prasad,' and 'kalapurusha' were felt to be untranslatable for which equivalent word in English or the Odia words had to be used. What's more, the rhythms noticed in the original Odia poetry have been lost and replaced by suitable rhythms in its respective English translation. Similarly, in certain cases, equivalent expressions for the figures of speech, collocations, idiomatic expressions and adjectival phrases have been used. The rephrasing and restructuring of sentences have also been done in some poems keeping in mind the linguistic properties and constraints of the target language.

CONTENTS

In Search of Water	13
The Monologue of Wind	18
The Inflamed Fire	20
A Word for the Earth	22
The Song of the Hills	24
Treasures of Quarry	26
The Feathered Friends	29
The Agonized Cloud	31
Thinking Trees	33
A Sprig of Grass	35
The Shining Summer	37
The Dike on Spate	39
Fire of Stomach	41
The Starved	44
Celebrating Rice	46
Immolation	48
The Song of Lily-1	51
The Song of Lily-2	53
The Song of Lake Chilika-1	55
Basal Spring	57
Drought	60
The Test Range	63
One Evening in the Monsoon	64
When Farmers Commit Suicide	66
Scarecrow	68
The Lost Village	69
Mango Blossoms	71

In Search of Water

||1||
'Where is water? Water, water?
Looking for it....?'
Is it in the sparkling fountains at the lake?
Or in the downpour of rainy season?
Is it in the green lake of your eyes?
Or on the bank of your well-navigable heart?
Or is it only the illusory verdant braids of oasis here?
'After all, where is water?'

||2||
Many have become tired and even exhausted
Of running after this oasis —
Involved in cutting down trees; and burning forests.
Some have gone mad to destroy them.
Alas! They also go on asking about water!
They ask about the core of the cloud; about food grain;
and about leaves after all!
'But, where is water?'

||3||
After so many wars,
What more dreadful does the earth to experience?

People have been fighting against each other
for generations–
To acquire the lands;
And to acquire the wealth stored under it.
Now, they must fight for clean water—
Perhaps, the last war!

People walk for miles holding pots and pans for water.
Their eyes look colourless and gruel-like.
Only deserts become visible to them.
As if a drop of water won't spring
In the eyes reflecting the sky….
Water will vanish somewhere into underground.
You will be only left with broken pots;
Broken fate as well;
Broken-hearted, all will shout
'Where is water?'

||4||
This summer,
Everybody is panic thinking about water!
Since long swans and cranes have already turned their faces back
From the inhumed banks of the lakes
Those banks burn with the gun powder of the glaring hunters.
Lots of unseen pyres of the trees cut down.
Everywhere it is sun-burnt—
'Where is water?'

||5||
The river you see here
Once when gets flooded, it spreads its watery wings

Across the streets and towns.
The embankments of the hearts of people
Get whirl pooled,
Leaving an imprint of sandy valleys.
No lands on the earth anymore get stored deep in the eyes;
Inside the hearts,
Leaves only wounds like turbid flood water.

Now, the entire river is full of sand only.
Trucks loaded with sand from the rivers run breathlessly
To fill the ditches and decks.
Once there were water iris, lily and lotus there…
But not now!
Perhaps the moon will slowly forget their
Reflections in the water.
And will ask: 'Where are those flowers?'
'Where is water?'

||6||
While offering *srāddha* to my mother at my village,
With much difficulty,
I had to dip my head into the dirty water
Of the village pond —
Now, I am looking for a holy river.
Where shall I immerse my mother's collar bone?
Where is the holy river?
Where are the holy flows of Ganga or Sarayu?
I can see only the deceased skeletons of the rivers there.
Filled with the greenery of garbage?
'Where is water?'

||7||
You know what happened?
One province in our country claims that it is their water.
'Nobody can resist it from flowing down;
You have to open the gates to release water.'
Then, the other province reacts saying—
'No, not a drop of water will be released.
If necessary, we'll have blood bath—
Remember, the rivers of blood will flow;
But no rivers of water!'

Leaders start wayfaring protesting;
Crops get destroyed in some places;
Farmers commit suicide dreading at the fierce shadow of drought;
The thirsty lips of the cracked farmlands whimper—
'Where is water?'

||8||
Now, we're ready to use gun powder to set the clouds ablaze;
We're ready to set gun powder to blow up the hills;
There's fire in the entire forest—spreading further;
No chance of putting out!
'Where is water?'

||9||
It is heard that all the rivers will be connected.
There will be no more drought and flood.
No more chance of lamenting the loss of harvesting;
No fetters of exploitation of the oppressor.
After long years, our children may try to understand
Line by line the meaning of the prayer *vande mātaram*.

By the time, they will hold the skeletons of the hills;
The bones of trees; sliced torso of the streams;
And then start searching for the rivers.
But, the rivers will already have been ceased back into
The primitive hills and valleys,
Where they had once originated.
Only you can hear the echo—
'Where is water?'

||10||
Water goes down and down to the deeper recesses of the earth;
To the abyss unknown;
No more water in the horizon lying under eyes;
Only sand covered valleys—
The burning desert, full of outcry—
'Where is water? Where…?'

- *Srāddha* is a Vedic ritual performed in commemorating the birth anniversary of the dead person in a family.

The Monologue of Wind

The wind told: 'I don't have strength and support;
Just now, came running from the pyre
Where a newlywed bride was made to burn hurriedly;
I came by the drums of bitumen boiling—
Emitting foul smell and making me breathless.

No, it cannot be tolerated— this scene, this smell!
There were green braids of paddy stalks gulping milk.'
While binding them,
The wind was limping like a feeble bitch—
As if it was going to groan finally.

The wind told: 'Nod the head.... swing all along.'
But, where is the place to sing the lories?
Already returned from visiting layered
and torn hills and blunt trees.
Where were the leaves in the trees to mourn?
The skeletons of many poems were lying
On the side of the streams flowing weakly.

The wind told: 'Yes.... sometimes
I'm available with the clouds.
If I feel like, I sit on the wings of the storks.
For quite a moment, I go to the thickly grown

Millet and sesame fields.
There, the birds fly away as soon as possible.
I wish I were with them.
To swing in their nests… patting the soft wings
Of their babies with love.
But, they also look for water in the decaying river banks.'

The wind told: 'Although I don't have any land or country,
In the drenched rainy days,
I help burning the glaring pyre of the
Young man who had to sacrifice
In the hands of the mafias,
And simultaneously carrying the fragrance
Of jasmine and mango blossoms.'

'In the autumn, the paddy stalks ready to gulp milk.
The fresh white kans grass …. the crepe jasmine
Touch the lilies softly….
The spring comes and goes unnoticed.
But the stolen season and I set aflame in body and mind.
The seasons look like a homeless widow.'
The wind told: 'I am unable to tolerate the barbaric
negligence;
Acts disastrously owing to the consequences;
I lose control over it.
To see the shadow of draught in the wide-stretched lands,
I get heart-broken;
Stay back in great remorse.
The soft voice that prays to the lord;
That is heard like the mantras or a hymn.
Trying to look for survival again and again,
Or else, the soul would become unmoved for long.'

The Inflamed Fire

To which people use as sport in Shravasti;
Dice on board rolls— they are all fire!
The fire is set ablaze, but the whole city is
Dipped in darkness!

Aren't you aware`
That you're in a trench of gunpowder?
Unable to know that you're moving on;
Uncountable trenches of gunpowder;
You're unable to know!

This fire once had come from that forest.
From the people of the caves sitting on fire,
And to feel the warmth.
From there, it went to the hearth;
Helped emitting the essence of rice boiling—
This fire had made us relished; showed us sympathy;
And gave vent to hunger a way.

Burnt as the wicker in the evening,
Offered for the gods and goddesses supposed to be
On the other side of the sky;
In the altars ... in the holy altars,
We prayed to them giving lots of names.
Offered our thanks;
Saying that let all the plights should be burnt—
Sin, heat and suffering.
Prayed that 'Let the world be enlightened;

Oh, the blue space of consciousness—
Give us cloud; give us corns;
And give us a glimpse of light to our villages.'

I have seen this fire getting inflamed
In the furnace as it swings its flames;
Also in lots of lamps... in the burning sticks
Getting brighter to bless someone
To let some go in light
Getting rid of their arrival amidst darkness.

Wherever this fire flared,
It got glistened.
However, today this fire
When travels from place to place,
Licks up the lives of the creatures –
Almost like jumping over here and there;
And grazing out whatever comes on the way.
Is this the same fire that started burning
Spreading all across and started
Reigning the macabre darkness,
In all directions along the horizon,
Burnt into ashes?
Buddha of Bamian and the steel buildings of Pentagon.

Will today a saint plan to sear him in this fire
In order to turn flesh and bone to sacred ash?
And spread in the garden of Shravasti
Where there will be sparkling flowers?
If that is not inflamed
In the lamp post of the heart,
Then the entire civilization will be inhumed
And the sun will drop drown by being cooler!

A Word for the Earth

I have been bearing the burden
Oh mother earth! I'm indebted
Lifelong have I been carrying this burden.
Where is time in life?
It is too short to payback your debts.

Here, I owe you a lot
I owe to this earth, water and air…. I owe a lot
To these trees and herbs;
To these stars and planets …. to monsoon and autumn.
The feelings of people-known and unknown;
The continuous flow of spirit of the ancestors
In this blood till now.

The safe veil of mother's saree;
The fragrant life of love of the beloved;
This whimsical life is in bond
With the lively touch of the sweet sound
Of her— makes me indebted to me.
Tell me how I can pay back the debt to all these…?

Here, the sun and the moon sparkle and glisten
In eyes and souls;
The rivers; the drops of rain become drops of blood
Flow in the arteries and veins.
The wind blows flooded
In the hearts through nostrils;

Through the juice of flowers
And leaves efflux through them
To reach in my bones and ribs.

I offer fire, water and homage for the liberation of the soul
Of the ancestors.
I move all along from Puri to Prayag
I put the collar bone of my father in this holy water.
This earth has been carrying me either on its head or shoulder.
How can I pay back its debt of her?
Only I can be a loanee of so much from them
Even serving for hundreds of autumn
Are not enough to negotiate.

The Song of the Hills

You go on telling the tales of the hills
Of the golden valley.
Those hills, their green breasts release the transparent
Streams of the springs, like the flow of milk.
These hills, the inn of the nomadic patches of clouds.
These hills, their bosoms are the safe haven for birds.
These hills that are like the humps on camels—
Each one is like the antique decorations of utensils.

Do you know? In the fresh heart of the forest products,
The soft skeleton of the streams
Along with the torso of the cloud
And in the patches of the garden
That gets stirred in the blood red setting sun
Only to make the last picnic
In the feinted moonlit yard.

In the flow of the music of anklet,
Poetry blossom near your reflection—
Image… symbol…. the poets will stir your poetry entirely
In the forest of sāl in Shravasti?

Before getting scattered,
These hills may be Bafalmali or it is Niyamgiri;
It is Gandhamradan or Bhaleri and Soleri
Will listen to the music of dollar or euro
Till they become deaf, bumb and blind;

Only teeth look sharp
And the tongue sparkles red.

Being the boss, you command sitting on your throne.
If anybody opens his mouth,
Then you will lose your fingers, hands
And even your head.
In the tinkling sound of dollar or euro,
You mark the wheel of development
To roll… singing the song of iron and nickel;
And to get immersed in happiness of people.
This explosion… these arrangements of displacement!

Which peak of the forests is in target after this?
Which twisted hill that looks like
The humps of a camel to you?
Which sunrise and sunset or the colourful rainbow?
In the heart and soul of the leaves which spring
Experience the last rain?

Maybe you will see
That on the wings of dead clouds;
The sparkles of the setting sun;
In the yards of the feinted moonlight;
There are heaps of skeletons of different people.
The flesh and bones are scattered
And there, you will sing the song of the setting sun.

Treasures of the Quarry

Go on digging more and more.
Let there be the beating of drums and cymbals and loud applause too.
The womb of the mines may not be exhausted with this.
So, go on digging till the centre of the earth;
Or till you get exhausted,
Go on digging.

Do you think that there would be a flow of clean water streams
When the mines are getting dug?
Or is it possible to find out
The body of unclad water streams?
Or the skeletons of the forest treasures?

It may be Toshali or Vaishali;
Or even the island of Jambu;
Everywhere, there is the *yajna* of progress.
The horse of *yajna* of progress
Marches ahead all the moment;
The so called chariot of progress
Clatters and echoes on your chest.
No way you've the guts to check it.

The animal kingdom of the land of forest,
Ranging from loincloth worn
To safari clad so called white elephants,

Hare, monkey and fox
Up to the flatterers at the chieftains' court;
Everybody gets the lion's share;
Everybody is affluent illegally.
For the so called bosses, every season is a golden season.
Season of harvest…. mild smile protracting
The decent manifestations of the body of such bosses
Also make them look affluent.

After all, what comes out of the mines?
Who cares about stones and cretaceous pebbles?
Comes out the valuable marble, mica and nickel;
Diamond stones and gems;
Many such inestimable things.

Fill their sacs, they go on collecting in a hurry
Before other coveters find them.
The capitalist, the industrialists—
Just like the sharp claws
Go on snatching them from the stock
And go on earning dollar, yen and rubble.
Everybody is affluent, belly full
And their pockets are full too.

Look at the procession of the dead clouds.
In the arête of the bald hill
Water has sunk down the earth.
Slowly, hands are unable to reach it.
While looking at the digging of the sites of mines,
You forget your food and drink
Because you are waiting to see the miracles of wealth
From the mines which is yet to come!

> Listen to me my dears—
> 'Henceforth, the skeletons of wind and cloud
> Will come out from the mines;
> And then the country's skeleton.
> You may not startle to see them
> That the coffin will be waiting
> To carry your skeleton too.'

- *Yajna* is one of the best Hindu practices done on the holy occasions with enchanting Vedic mantras before the sacred fire placed in a sanctified earthen pit in which pure ghee and other relevant ingredients are offered with great devotion.

The Feathered Friends

Like every year, this year
The Siberian travelling birds are getting ready
From lake Chilka to go back—
Determining the directions and the peaks;
Planning to go back to the green plains of Siberia.
Slowly, Chilka becomes a feinted blue lake,
Like So-morir of Kashmir and Logtak of Manipur
Now, smouldering of the poisonous gun powder
Making the sky suffocated.

Now, no place is left without the fetters of fire…
The strong net of the blood-thirsty eyes of
The hunters are inflamed everywhere.
The prawn mafias are included too.

Injured in the bullets and bayonets,
The injured birds
(Doubtful whether from Chilka or Siberia)
Open their wings to escape
As they become tired of breathing and drinking.
The poison of the gun powder—
They get thirsty… throat gets dried up
The sky is red hot in the gun powder.
The wings of the birds get burnt.

The entire earth, trees, forests and space,
The sky and the ground belong to the birds.

If the birds ask:
'We are not only the birds of Chilka or Siberia!
We're spread in the world.
But is there any blue space spread across
Where we all can be accommodated –
In a dense hole or any place; may be peaks or flights;
Any alight or descent for us?'

The Agonized Cloud

The clouds love to be in the sky,
To swing in the space like small children
Whenever they feel like.
They may take rest somewhere
In the top of the horizon
Or in the lonely mountains;
Connect stories with the stars and galaxies
Or with the hollowness,
The whole night....
The sky feels shy at this keeping herself in the lee.

The patches of multicoloured clouds
Form a flock of the peaceful nomads?
The cranes, swans, open bill or kites
While flying, they touch the wings of the clouds happily.
At times, touch the kites of children too.

Sitting in the palanquin of wind,
The clouds drop in the valleys
On the souls of the cracked earth.... dead grass,
And those which are thirsty.
Bundles of clouds in thousand flows,
Kiss the earth as if there is a great kindness
Of wetness flows out of the blue palm...

Henceforth, some conspirators
Think of holding the wings of the clouds
And then cut them off
With their stainless steel knives.
Stifle the neck of the clouds;
Set them ablaze with the gun powder;
And then sleep uninterrupted
On the bed of the skeletons of blue hills and green trees.

Can the patches of cloud now rest their cheeks
And look at the distant fields wearing the ornaments of paddy stalks?
Or sailing of the paper boats by the naughty children?
The silvery scaled anklets of the earth and the rivers...
The blood red sun that bejewels its head
With a patch of vermillion mark,
Look at the rheumy eyelids of the deserts
Will it leave the place crying?

The cloud never giggles... sees it gets ready
To bend upon the earth... like a bright gaze
Of the golden dazzle of lightening that spreads across
And thus, the earth is filled with
The fragrance of its breathe.

Thinking Trees

|| 1 ||
Cutting across the hills, they have already
Reached the forest of sāl trees
Now, it's the turn for cutting them down;
Like the village folk offering
One head each day to the demon,
Each of these trees will have to sacrifice before them
And have to fall down every day.

Think about these trees;
About their laps full of stems and branches;
The soft and cool shadow they provide
Just like the drape of mother's saree
They provide solace.
But, do these assassinators understand this?

These assassinators get tired of stinging the trees;
Still then these trees stretch their aprons of cool shade
To clean the sweats of their bodies
Still then, the trees are filled with unfathomable adoration!

|| 2 ||
Before falling down, the trees go on speaking
"See, you don't understand at all;
If I am never there, in which branches will you sit?
Can you feel the wind pluck the swift light of March?"

While cutting, you will see that
Both your body and mind get burnt
In the terrible heat ... entire Srabasti gets burnt
Drops of blood of the setting sun
Chintz on the corpse of Chaitali.

While cutting, you will see that
You've cut your own feet
Or, you turn to become defunct, diseased
And neither the earth would have the strength
To take you into her lap
Nor it will have anywhere a patch of soft and cool shade.

The sky will look sharp like the sword of stainless steel
But maybe, for me it squeezed out
Some drops of blue drops for me only.

By cutting the hills, they....!

A Sprig of Grass

Destined to get trampled under feet
Whatever grass is left
Though we know it to be so soft and smooth.

Although mutilated, mounds of grass
Move ahead till the last patch is found on the earth.
Still it endeavours to spread on the earth
To make it look fresh.

For years together, it has not become tired;
Run ahead stumbling again and again;
Your hands and feet may become defunct,
But, they are never tired.

They never care for the so called heat of sun
Or stormy rain;
Gossip even in the desert
As if planning to spread the tapestry of greenery all over.
Wipe out your travel sore.
The tiresome body and mind
And form the dome of green all around.
Although your shoes step over them,
They remain fearless and careless;
They know that they are destined to be trampled
And still dream of fresh revival.

No sun or the dews can leave
These fresh and soft grown grass undazzled
No cloud or the rainbow can leave them
Without tuning them with their colours.

Still you think them to be mere sprig of grass till now?

The Shining Summer

Summer never repents
Although the door of the green forest is closed
When he arrived,
The doors and windows of the cities started closing
Instead of calling him as the sparkles of silver and gold
People went on grumbling—
"Why doesn't it turns blind, this burnt- faced sun!"
Defamed for causing sun-stroke and untimely death too.

What would this sunlight do?
Blindly gulp the castigation
While making an effort to take rest in the mango orchard.
Its head was crashed against the bulk of the mango tree.
What! Holding its blood stained forehead,
It thought whether it would rush into the cave
Of the hill searching for shadow!
While searching for shadow, a little rest, and sleep,
It found the flesh and bone of the hill lay scattered.
Beside it fallen the unclad
And helpless body of the water stream.
The sunlight got suffocated
In the layered dust spread everywhere
Almost sobbing with its pale face,
In its border of feint-look and choked breathe.

Being thirsty searching for some water,
It went along the river bank.

But, alas! There is no flight of a single crane or kingfisher.
The feeble stream of water was almost hidden
In the widespread sand
Emitting foul smell,
The throat of the sunlight was getting dried up
Would it burst out after all?

Before being lifeless and about to lose sense, it saw
A patch of bulky black cloud gets uddered
From the north-east sky... cold wind blows
Moving along rapidly with drops of water.
The exhausted sunlight opened its eyes;
Felt as if somebody has daubed
The cool fragrance and salve
All along its body
Is it wind or cloud?

The Dike on Spate

Cannot check the river in spate
Every year, this dike gets damaged.
The fierce flow of water of the river
Licks out houses and buildings; plants and trees;
Fields and grains;
Grounds filled with silt or grazed with sand
Of the streets and corners of Shreebasti.

Then, it accounts for dripping of tear
From the eyes and break the embankment of
The bones of the chest;
Turns blood into water;
And makes so deep an unseen dike
That it falls and rises from the over-flooded spirit
Thus making him lick like old oxen
The incurable injuries of loss.

After that come the builders of the nation
In boats and flights,
Wearing safari and suit
Flatterers and volunteers arrive
With spade and relief packets;
First-aid and tool box to repair the face of the dike;
Start measuring the length and breadth
In order to find out ways of many twists and
manipulations

Make efforts to measure the fathom and width
Of injury made by the dike.

Then, although it throws
The nation behind the bars of loan;
Prepare a list of many false casualties and damages
From which the blood and tear of the victims flow down
In order to garnish the bread of the so called great people
With ghee and honey.

Then people with dried up bellies
Stand at the face of the dike;
With dried up cheeks too.
Look at the sand covered fields of corn
And look at the poverty-stricken body
In the reflections of the flood water;
Startled to think if it is their images
Or the images of some skeletons and ghosts!

The Fire of the Stomach

Never now, it is since long
This hunger has made its space in the dense forest.
Everybody is frightened at its roaring—
It has gulped trees and plants; animals and birds;
The flesh and blood of human beings,
It eructs and like a dumb thick-bodied deity
Present in the dark sanctum sanctorum
This hunger keeps sitting fearlessly.

Have not you seen
The way it looks when it stares?
It does not look like the dried up shuck of mango
Or like a mango stone
Or like the pale eyes of the fasters
Have not you seen the flame of the stomach?

Hunger neither has brain nor heart;
Only it has a big gape
In which there is a sharp tongue,
A set of rugged sharp teeth.
It moves like the almighty God;
Continues for centuries,
Since the time of barren land of the ninth king,
Till the seeds of tamarind and mango stone
Or rotten and dried up meat
Or rice available at the drain pipe of the five star hotels.

This hunger moves holding the broken pitchers and
potsherd
From Kashipur to the entire area

Hunger:
Breaks the slumber of the trees;
Squeezes all juice and honey
From the mango blossoms;
From the cooing of the blackbird
To the lips of the ripened red mango.

Like a tantric, this hunger begs
The blood of a virgin; heart of a baby;
Muscles of a young man;
Varieties of immolation
Does this hunger wishes to become immortal
Before some unusual deity?
This hunger rushes into the flowers like kurei and alasi
Enters into the saffron.
Green poison spreads in its sting
And clings in the joints of the bones
In the pits of the eyes;
And slumbers carelessly in the arena of the ribs
Of the hungry people.

In the dead streams or the turbid water,
The sun and the moon are seen to them.
They can see the white substance in mango stones
Look like handful of rice or pieces of bread.
The hungry feel as if they are like butter and honey for
them.

Hunger comes out there with dynamite, spade and axe;
Bulldozer, scissors and bill hock
To cut the peacock like neck of the water streams.
The heart of the deer in the forest
They cut the hills and valleys into pieces;
Part by part, just like the butcher removes the skin
And slices huge pieces of flesh and bone.
From the rumps and navels
Hunger alights amongst the touts, butchers and mafias.

At that time, hunger becomes red hot like the sun,
Just like a demonic pandemic, it pierces into the hole of
utter darkness,
And returns with the skulls, intestines, eyes and skeletons
Of the beautiful valley.

Hunger brightens steel, aluminium, and diamond rubbing
And polishing; then moves along the world in the flights
Provided by multinational companies;
Wears expensive suits and shoes measured in dollar and
rubble
Giving the slogan of globalization.

This hunger attempts at digging innumerable holes
At some grey coloured unusual place
To bury the skulls, intestine, eyes and skeletons;
And at that time, the villains spread around
The labyrinth of the game
Or start playing some new game of dice.

The Starved

||1||
Belly is not filled with poetry.
Conversely, poetry cannot provide livelihood.
Somebody had told this
That the thought of food is wonderful.
While saying so, the poet cuts the branch in which he sits
And even cuts the feet in which he stands.

Belly is in its own way whereas poetry
Takes its own way as well.
Sometimes do they meet
On the bank of the flooded river
May be at Ujjaini or at Shreevasti or so.

||2||
The so called paragon's description loses
All its aesthetics near
A wrinkled or drained belly which is already dried up;
The moon loses its metaphor
May be renamed as a burnt chapatti by some poets.
Sometimes, the mango seed
Which is sealed in mango stone
Gains value for the starved folk.

||3||
Although all these dramas are only for this tiny belly
There is a saying that it is not an offence to commit sin

To fill this empty belly.
People say that there is food for everyone.
But, the story of empty stomach is age old;
Still then, it continues...
Babies born from the wombs are sold to make ends meet.
Passionate after the deal of those so called flesh!

||4||

This belly of the starved may not be visible
In the dome of the tattered clothes
That is stitched several times to look like maps.
But, their dismal labour in all seasons,
Their bodies get bent while sweating profusely.
Bones are counted; ribs look like sticks;
Marks of being lashed at the back
Speak a lot about the reality of their small empty bellies.

||5||

Look at the demolition of their world in the supercyclone.
The broken embankments of the fierce dance of the
Flooded rivers,
Or the cracked and gaped farmlands.
Look at the naked and cold hearth;
Look at the coming out of their intestines
In the stampede at the relief camps;
Look at the dead bodies of farmers
Committed suicide for being unable to pay back the loan,
Or the death account of the persons owing to starvation.
Look at their eyeballs—
The universal incarnation of the would be worth nothing
As the lord himself would be perturbed or even startled
To see all these!

Celebrating Rice

This rice is the source of the bright smile of a baby
Causing the holy and white bones look fresh.

The smell that emanates from the pot on the hearth.
Its raised steam is full of the smell of life.
The smell of the earth in the shower of the early monsoon
Makes us feel the warmth of the blood in arteries
Or is it the smell of hunger?

Felt as if the milk of mother earth;
Her closeness of affection gets soaked
And boils over as the
Sweet smelling white fresh rice.

In a pot full of rice, the dreadful bones of hunger
Of the procession of the deceased,
The victims of flood relief stampede.
The groaning of the sick;
The hunger of this small belly
Digs furrows that cordate across the heart
In the pale eyeballs… in empty stomachs—
Where there is utter darkness.

Only a pot of rice is noticed in hallucination
For that pot of rice.
All those slavery, forced labourer, and exploitation

All those give and take
Dreams, nightmares, buffer stocks and deaths too.

How unreachable is the sky of our hunger?
Can any light touch it?
Listen to me if you ask at all—
Rice is the only answer for that.

This rice tears darkness into pieces
Makes the nights starry
After gulping the tears and breaths or blood
Feels like rice is taste; rice is fragrance; rice is honey;
And rice is celebration.

Immolation

|| 1 ||

Immolation is truth! This immolation does not
Understand the story of hunger of anybody;
No care for the language of diligence;
This has come down to the pages of history
Since human being knows the use of weapons;
Enjoys the flavour of the liver of some creatures.
Blood spilled in the ground of this earth are
Only the bloods of immolation.
Yes, it is immolation.

|| 2 ||

Do the deities of the temple ask us to immolate?
Do they ask us our blood?
We offer a hen or goat, immolate them.
In the pretext of ritual,
We are pushed towards the firth of decay.
That day, the black blood of Mahisasur had become
Flowers at the feet of the goddess.
Today, at the time of her immersion ceremony,
The streets and valleys became red
With the explosion of bombs and stabbing;
We bathe our deities in the temples, mosques or churches
In that blood—
But, whose blood is this?
Whose immolation these could be?

|| 3 ||
Do you know the history of Hastinapur or Magadh?
In every war, there was an incident of immolation.
Ranging from the river of blood
That flew along Kurukhetra
Or the flow of blood at river Daya.
There, father sailed across the river of blood with dead body of his son;
Here, the blood red dusk extends to the
Horizon of renunciation.

|| 4 ||
Don't ask— who is the victor and who is the victim?
Neither the earth nor the blood knows
That this is immolation.
Can a king building monument support immolation?
Can a labourer sweating at the furnace
Or a farmer harvesting in the field
Be the victims of immolation of anybody?

The so called hunter
Makes the dove a victim of immolation;
May be the Bhopal gas tragedy
Or the earthquake at Lisbon or Latur;
Or the forest fire that makes lives sacrifice
Making each moment sensitive;
Don't ask me who is the immolator there?

|| 5 ||
Forget the story of Hastinapur or Magadh;
Think about the massacre at Jaliwanawalabag;
Or about the dead bodies in the Burla power channel
The story of crucifixion of the son of the lord;

The assassination of the man of
The millennium at the prayer;
Victims of hunger whether in Ethiopia or Kalahandi
Are their pensive eyeballs so different?
There goes immolation at every moment.

|| 6 ||
Is this immolation a sacrificial altar
Of the labyrinth of multiple defensive walls?
Are the skeletons of babies recovered from
The Maninag hills
A part of this kind of sacrifice?
Even the newlywed brides and now soil, water, wind —
All of you have to get ready to be sacrificed —
We are already entangled in the war of scud-patriot;
Of Star war, and many more —
We celebrate the festival of sacrifice;
But the last victim of this sacrifice is yet to be seen!

|| 7 ||
Let this immolation be auspicious.
Let a Konark be built out of this.
If sacrifice can clean stains from glory of humanity,
Then let's sacrifice.
If the blood red horizon can give birth to a beautiful sun,
Then, immolation is welcome.
Let this immolation make the earth purer,
Holy and auspicious.

- Daya river is on the east of Bhubaneswar, historically known for the Kalinga war.
- Burla power channel remains in news for people die in its strong current.
- Kalahandi is a district in Odisha.
- Maninag hills in in the district of Nayagarh.

The Song of Lily-1

Inhumed all these
Get buried
When the sound of the trucks full of sand
Is heard all day and night;
When stone pieces get crushed
And grinded to form concrete
Can these make the lily be ecstatic in the full moon night?

Blossomed in the dirty dump mud
But, where is lily?
Get buried these flowers.
But, strangely the starry nights,
Full-moon nights; sleeps and dreams;
Colours and fragrance never get buried.

Walls are erected;
New walls of mosaic and marble of new apartments
In the clusters of towering sky scrappers
The flowers; the sky;
And even scotch grass lose their existence?

This lily is a metaphor for the young girl;
Bunches of lilies on festivals adorn the pandals;
Its open white petals are metaphors for
The half-open lips of the young girl,
The new bride in a lilyless city

Lives with her husband —
Does she lament your loss?

The innocent and soft girl —
Her neck gets stifled within the four walls
Of the so called building.
Her eyes and heartbeats get attuned to mosaic and marble.
Then, who cares about lilies?

Everything gets buried!

The Song of Lily-2

That was the dawn of a full moon night
When I was passing along the village pond silently.
My nose tip could sense of those lilies
And heard them gossiping.

The most talkative lily
Nodded and said: "See that poet is passing.
He writes poems on lily and lotus...
He wrote that everything is buried—
The pools are buried;
The streams bearing lilies and lotuses are buried;
Sleeps and dreams; memories and full moon nights are buried
Buried amidst the sand and concrete crowded apartments."

"Yes, he had given us a metaphor
Of the young girls who pluck bundles of lilies
Colour poured over their lips and their tempting looks
As the beloved ones."
Spoke out both the green and red lilies uncontrollably;
The blue and still water got bobbed in their giggles.

In the moon light… getting enchanted
When I attempted a step forward,
The white lily said, "Listen oh poet, in their rebirth,

These spirits of the human beings
While moving over the land
Would definitely travel over the stars and planets…
Or Move along the crowding towers of mosaic and concrete;
One day, they would ask sobbing –
Where are those hills and trees… the forests?
Where are those full moon nights
Reflected in the pool full of lilies?

Getting out of these apartments,
They will look for lilies… and the reflection of the moon,
Not only in the water but also in their eyes, in minds and in their bosoms
And will say: 'There is no pool, therefore no lilies;
And no full moon night as well.
The moonlit night feels lifeless
Without the fragrance of lilies.
Hey poet, still then don't get disheartened.'

The Song of Lake Chilika-1

The water in you no more looks blue.
There is no reflection of any swans.
Water looks pale in the blood of the preyed creatures.

In the deafening sound of the gunfire,
Ears become defunct
As the flesh of the swan is seen hung down the bayonets.

Before the hornbill flies shedding plumes…
Before shedding tears from the eyes of the princess…
The fish and the swans become blind…
Before the soft meeting and mating of the couples;
Before the night comes to an end,
Arrows slip from the bows of the hunter
To pierce their soft and silken bodies.

The bride named Jai once had been to her in-laws
Noticed while sailing across the lake
That there was no rain or storm.
But, she found that the half burnt corpse was floating
Looked almost like her!
Floated near the canyon where
There was unfathomable water.
She was frightened as the sailor sailed slowly.

The boat that is built in the bones of the swans
Carries hundreds of dead birds.
The beating of their wings becomes less
Causing to bleed from some part of my heart—
I get drowned in the deep canyon.

As if the fleshes that are hung down the bayonet
Are like the pieces of my heart?

- Jai is a reference to the popular folktale of Kalijai rendered as a ballad by famous Odia poet Godabarish Mishra.

Basal Spring

Breaking the crowd of all varieties of apartments,
Jumping across the road of bitumen
And concrete in vehicles
We reached at the basal spring.
There was an adventure of the cloud
In the streets and fairs.
Half of the leaves were lost in the trees
Making them look bony and helpless there.
The surrounding dry trunks of
The trees look grey and boiled.
Where is the spring here?
There is no breeze even in the early March.
Wonderfully secluded!

No shade. No bustling of leaves.
No flight of kingfishers or kites;
No sound of cuckoos.
Only the rampant sound of the horns of vehicles,
And a few aeroplanes circling round the sky,
Below it, there are crossroads and bends on the road
having lots of hoardings—
Advertising wine, saree, cell phone,
And many sundry products.
A half embedded pool having some dry stems of white lily
There are cracked farmlands burning like hearth,
Making us feel very lonely and lifeless.

Once we had cycled up to the basal spring
That day, with the untimely rain, the sky was looking
splendid with rainbow;
That spring was like our childhood and teenage—
Quite innocent and dreamy
Then, there was politeness both in grass and wind;
Everywhere coconuts, mango, neem and tamarind
Made us feel as if only trees can form the horizons.
The sleepy nights under the canopy of the stars
Were deeper and comfortable.

That green village was full of
Yellow oleander, moonbeam,
White tulip and lemonwood flower.
The fragrance of the mango blossoms—
It seemed as if the spring was
The eternal inhabitant of that place.
Spread its bed and slumbers happily.

The powerful sultry and layers of dust;
The burning bitumen yielding smell;
Suddenly arrived carrying the tired smoke of the kiln.
Once this wind was swinging happily in
The dense branches of trees
Translating the unexpressed languages of the damsels
In letters carrying the essence of coral jasmine
Speeding up swiftly like and stubborn child.

But now, that wind is utterly heckled
And moved to some place
To extinguish the cremation of a bride
The dove mourns over it; the wing sobs;
Everybody was tired and jaded.

We talked with a symphony of agony
That since the spring vanished,
The cuckoos and black-hooded oriole also vanished.
The trees shade leaves to directly arrive at the summer.
All our travels to be accomplished in the dire summer!
Sweating, we lost the path.
We are tired of looking for the basal spring.
Now the fresh white forehead of the dawn;
Its starry canopies at night—
All vanished.

Drought

Drought is simply aridity.
The soil gets cracked in the macabre whimper.
Bodies get baked in the hot pan of the strong sun.

There's oasis in his dreadful look;
Endless thirst in his lips of desert;
Trees and plants dry up in its treachery;
Sucks the blood and flesh from the body;
And marrow from the bones.

The green cornfield withers.
When steps on it, the earth falls apart.
Looks like the dried and expanded ribs—
Fathomless fissures in the heart of the farmer.
Thus, he benevolently looks for a vial of poison
Or, a rope to hang him to death.
His better half gets ready
To break the bangles of her hands.
Preparing the death procession,
Where the echo of the cry of her children is heard.

Wearing the dead garland of tattered clouds
The *kalapurush* comes down from the distant shadow;
Stepping on the number of half effaced embroideries.

x   x   x

The white saree like clouds turn into pieces and flies away.
In the pale crematorium of the sky,
The sun with a sharp axe is ready
To sacrifice the virgin cloud.

The moon: like a fresh dead skull
Stars: a group of seekers of alms
Night: a city of apparitions
The cracked cornfields: the skeleton of humans

There is fire
All the plants and trees are burnt…
The whole blueness of the sky
Wallows along with the soft glory of the soil.

x   x   x

The sky looks like the hollow belly under the skeleton;
The treasured greenness of the deceased
Or bony trees are sucked.
In the season of monsoon, there is sparkling sun,
Ready to slice off the throat of the hay stalks.

The one you call as the hay stalks
Are but the crumbed fingers
Of uncountable hungry people.
The one you name as the cracked fields
Are but the symbols of the helpless hearts,
Or the dried breast of a hungry mother
That is still sucked by the crazy baby.

But, there those who are in the flood of food
Seated in the cushions
And full of milk and honey.
Can they realize the agony of the scorching hunger

That makes the bones and flesh turn into pieces?
There, the door of the silky smooth heart is closed for all.
Here, the worms of drought spread poison
And cut the bones and flesh.

Still the skeletons turn to become soil;
Silt of the corn fields
Making us smell life.

The flood will flow;
The rain will shower;
But all in false speeches
In the tears of pretention,
Some will float on honey and ghee
Whereas some others' skeletons get crucified —
Become the tools of bier.

The Test Range

I'm stood on the heap of gunpowder
Since long—
No chance of shedding tear!
It got evaporated and lost in the sky.

Now, I'm ready to be sacrificed.
Ready to be in the cobweb of controversy.
Is it the smoke of the gun powder or cloud there?
Why do the rays of the sun look like the spatters of blood?
The sun looks red although it's not the sunset.
Or has somebody stifle the torso of the swans of the cloud.

The moon looks worried
To see as if dissected dead body of a child
Hung down a blunt branch.

One Evening in the Monsoon

One evening in the monsoon
I searched for the ridge gourd and cucumber flowers
Sang the song of them?
Looked for the lilies in the gradually
Inhumed small village pond.

In between the cement concrete houses,
A thatched house was visible.
I looked for the creepers of ridge gourd
And cucumber on its roof.
Looked for the pond shining in the moonlit
Where I expected lilies to gossip.

I know that the flowers of ridge gourd have no smell
But, they are the golden blossoms.
Then, in the approach of evening and moonlit night,
I looked for my blameless beautiful beloved
In the bunches of ridge gourd flowers.
But alas! It is darkened, faded and gone.
Still I searched for the maiden
Whom I had given a bunch of lilies
On a festive occasion—
Her bright smile like a full-blossomed lily
Plait of hair like a snake or like a garland of lilies
Looked for her innocent and pure smile
Amidst the bunch of blossomed lilies.

Searching for *Prasad*—
The sweet smell of the mash of fried rice,
Jaggery and cucumber
The grace of the goddess was felt there.
In my small village—
However, I looked for life amidst the lost paddy fields
Where a loanee farmer died of drinking pesticides
Looked for the monsoon evening that settles
In his lifeless eyes,
Just like a burnt wick of the lamp that slowly
Put out unnoticed.

When the Farmers Commit Suicide...

Not only in the monsoon but also throughout the year,
New information reaches regarding
How the dead bodies of them are found
In the middle of the corn fields.
Why do they commit suicide
In those impervious cornfields?
Is it their protest against the lord for destroying their golden lands?
Do they leave this corporeal frame in such desolated lands
To make their voices echo at the Creator?

Lest somebody would call them timid
Looking at their impotent eyes.
The agonized, infirm and wrinkle- faced farmers
Don't go to buy poison in the market
Because the illusions of friends and families
Would hinder them from making their voices
Reach the Creator.

Drought waits for them holding the black noose
At the cornfield where the corn stalks look like
Broken and feeble beings
Drying up at par with those farmers
As both of them die— the crops and the farmers.

This suicide follows the speeches of moralists
The protests of the opposition party
And the reaffirmation of the people in power
To connect the rivers; to do this and that;
The atheists will talk of the prefixed fate—
The result of the actions of the previous life!

Scarecrow

No need of making a scarecrow for the destroyed crops.
It would have guarded if
There were greeneries full in the fields.
In the burden of loan,
Now he himself has become a scarecrow
Who is ready to drive the vacuum—
Realize nothingness in the worm eaten hay stalks.
His head is bald like the corn field.
And the remaining lock of hair looks grey.
The cracked heals and the ribs look like the cracked field.

The dead farmer with his fresh suicide
In the midst of corn fields
Looks lifeless like a scarecrow.
A head as bald as the pitcher;
Eyes as black as carbon;
Torn clothes surround the body casually.
No chance of revival as the body is immovable;
No hot and wind blows along her body
As it used to blow along the cornfields.

Like the infirm scarecrow made of wicker,
The body parts of the farmer jiggles
Reflecting the endless suffering
Of the discontented soul;
Still then, it is perhaps ready to guard his field
Until it becomes cram of green hay stalks.

The Lost Village

There was a dense orchard—
Full of greenness of the tope;
Normal weather throughout the year;
Humans, animals and birds— all were devoid of stress.

The roar of the summer storm;
The vroom of the vehicles
Would never disturb the serenity
Never disturb the birds and animals
From countryside happiness.
Although alone, all are fearless, all in harmony.

The blackbird is free to sing full-throated
Alongside the village road
Having canopied with infinite spring.
The long-stretched paddy fields;
The celebration of mango and jackfruit in the
Bunch of branches interwoven.
All are silent as if sleeping casually—
The tailor, the passenger, bus driver and the tea-maker.
This is the land of stress-free sleep
Making me dream iceland, deserts, and pier
And the beautiful sky.
x x x
After thirty years, on my revisit,
The black bird was no more.
Only vehicles running

And random populous movements.
The cosy and shadowy tope has vanished.
The paddy fields, the jute forest, all are gone grey.
After the death of the black bird,
All are tuned to TVs and radios.
No bus comes to the stop slowly.
My downhearted self still looks for
The lost address of those days.

Mango Blossoms

Is your smell a sparkler
That pierces into my look and ignites my blood vessels?
Is it fire or the blazoning memories?
Burns or stings?
Does you fragrance enliven the sweet memories?

What is the relation of the clouds
With the mango blossoms?
But, once having a look at them
Both in the sky and in deep recesses of my heart
Blossoms of the clouds of hope germ unfathomable.

Not only do the clouds rise
In some green vacuity
(Or in fullness?)
Both body and mind get drenched?
I neither become dripping clouds
Nor the fragrant blossoms
Endeavour entirely to energize the earth and the air?

Black Eagle Books

www.blackeaglebooks.org
info@blackeaglebooks.org

Black Eagle Books, an independent publisher, was founded as a nonprofit organization in April, 2019. It is our mission to connect and engage the Indian diaspora and the world at large with the best of works of world literature published on a collaborative platform, with special emphasis on foregrounding Contemporary Classics and New Writing.

www.ingramcontent.com/pod-product-compliance
Lightning Source LLC
Chambersburg PA
CBHW030535080526
44585CB00014B/947